# CROCK POT CHICKEN RECIPES COOKBOOK

*+60 Quick & Easy Recipes and Dishes to Stay Healthy, and Find Your Well-Being*

# CROCK POT CHICKEN RECIPES COOKBOOK ........................ 1

## INTRODUCTION ................................................................. 6

- Chicken with Cranberries ............................................................ 8
- Chicken with Dried Beef ............................................................ 10
- Chicken With Garlic and Pineapple ........................................ 12
- Chicken with Grapes ................................................................. 14
- Chicken With Honey .................................................................. 16
- Chicken with Macaroni and Smoked Gouda Cheese .......... 18
- Chicken With Noodles, Slow Cooker ..................................... 20
- Chicken with Onions .................................................................. 23
- Chicken With Parsley Dumplings ........................................... 25
- Chicken With Pearl Onions and Mushrooms ....................... 27
- Chicken With Pineapple ........................................................... 29
- Chicken-Rice Casserole ............................................................ 31
- Chili Chicken ................................................................................ 33
- Chinese-Style Chicken and Vegetables ................................ 35
- Cornish Game Hens with Rice ................................................ 37
- Cornish Hens with Raisin Sauce ............................................. 38
- Country Captain Chicken Breasts .......................................... 40
- Country Chicken and Mushrooms ......................................... 42
- Country Club Chicken ............................................................... 43
- Cranberry Chicken ..................................................................... 45
- Cranberry Chicken II .................................................................. 47
- Cream Cheese Chicken ............................................................. 49
- Creamy Chicken and Artichokes ............................................ 51
- Creamy Italian Chicken ............................................................. 53
- Creole Chicken ............................................................................ 55
- Creole Chicken With Sausage ................................................. 57
- Crock Pot Chicken and Artichokes ........................................ 59
- Crock Pot Chicken And Dressing ........................................... 61
- Crock Pot Chicken Enchilada Hot Dish ................................. 63
- Crock Pot Chicken Enchiladas ................................................ 65
- Crock Pot Chicken Tortillas ..................................................... 67
- Crockpot Cassoulet ................................................................... 69
- Crockpot Chicken and Herb Dumplings ............................... 71
- Crockpot Chicken Barbecue ................................................... 73
- Crockpot Chicken Chili .............................................................. 75
- Crockpot Chicken Chow Mein ................................................ 77
- Crockpot Chicken Cordon Bleu .............................................. 79
- Crockpot Chicken Dinner ......................................................... 81
- Crockpot Chicken Drumsticks ................................................ 83
- Crockpot Chicken Fricassee Recipe ...................................... 85
- Crockpot Chicken Reuben Casserole ................................... 88

*Crockpot Chicken With Artichokes* ......................................................... *90*
*Crockpot Chicken with Dijon Mustard* .................................................... *92*
*Crockpot Chicken With Tomatoes* .......................................................... *94*
*Crockpot Cola Chicken* ............................................................................ *96*
*Crockpot Creole Chicken* ........................................................................ *97*
*Crockpot Herb Chicken With Stuffing* ..................................................... *99*
*Crockpot Italian-Style Chicken* ............................................................. *102*
*Crock Pot Lima Beans with Chicken* ..................................................... *104*
*Crockpot Pasta and Cheese Delight* ..................................................... *106*
*Debbie's Crockpot Chicken and Stuffing* .............................................. *108*
*Diana's Chicken a la King* ..................................................................... *111*
*Dilled Chicken with Veggies* ................................................................. *113*
*INGREDIENTS* ........................................................................................ *113*
*Don's Sweet and Sour Chicken* ............................................................. *115*
*Easy Cheesy Slow Cooker Chicken* ....................................................... *117*
*Easy Chicken Cacciatore* ....................................................................... *119*
CONCLUSION ............................................................................................... 121

# *INTRODUCTION*

Chicken is one of the most versatile ingredients when it comes to the family of meats. Healthy and tasty, you can add
it to almost any lunch or dinner dish that you can think of to make it a truly well-rounded meal. Indeed, chicken appears in almost every popular cuisine of the many cultures around the world, and if it is not in the main dish of that country, then it certainly has a place somewhere in day-to-day gastronomy. Yet due to the fact that it is such a widely used meat, there are

some individuals and families who might grow bored with having to prepare it for so many meals per night. They feel they have prepared almost every dish they can think of, or they do not know where to find other more innovative recipes to keep the meals fresh and new.
Crock Pot Chicken Recipes is the solution to that problem of the humdrum dinner.
Not only are there a handful of delicious meals that are easy to follow and come out wonderful, but these are also recipes that rely on one of the most helpful pieces of equipment a kitchen can feature: a crockpot. With this tool, you simply load it up with the ingredients that you need for the dish, turn the heat and timer settings to where they need to be according to your recipes, and walk away.

There's not much more to it! You can delight your family and your friends with these scrumptious recipes that will have them thinking you slaved in the kitchen for hours on end! When in reality, all you did was load your crockpot and have the foresight to prepare yourself with these exquisite meal ideas.

# Chicken with Cranberries

## INGREDIENTS

• 6 boneless, skinless chicken breasts • 1 small onion, chopped • 1 cup fresh cranberries • 1 teaspoon salt • 1/4 teaspoon ground cinnamon • 1/4 teaspoon ground ginger • 3 tablespoons brown sugar or honey • 1 cup orange juice • 3 tablespoons flour mixed with 2 tablespoons cold water

## PREPARATION

1. Place all ingredients, except flour and water mixture, in the slow cooker or Crock Pot. Cover and cook on low 6 to 7 hours, until chicken is tender. Add flour mixture in the last 15 to 20 minutes and cook until thickened. Taste and adjust seasonings.

2. Serves 4.

# Chicken with Dried Beef

## INGREDIENTS

- 1 jar dried beef, about 2 1/2 ounces, rinsed • 6 boneless chicken breast halves, skin removed • 6 slices bacon • 1/4 cup sour cream • 1/4 cup flour • 1 can cream of mushroom soup, undiluted • 2 to 3 tablespoons dry white wine, optional

## PREPARATION

1. On bottom of greased slow cooke, arrange dried beef. Wrap each piece of chicken with a strip of bacon; arrange on top of dried beef. In small bowl, combine sour cream and flour; add soup and wine, if using, and blend thoroughly. Pour over chicken mixture. Cover and cook on LOW for 6 to 8 hours.

2. Serves 6.

3. Serve with hot cooked rice and salad or potatoes and a green vegetable.

# Chicken With Garlic and Pineapple

## INGREDIENTS

- 3 1/2 pounds chicken
- 1 clove garlic, minced • sliced in syrup, reserve syrup • green onions, thinly sliced • tablespoon vinegar
- salt • pepper • 1/4 teaspoon ground ginger 1 cup chicken broth • 8 1/2 ounces pineapple, 4 ounces sliced water chestnuts, drained • 4 1/4 cup cornstarch • 1/4 cup soy sauce • 1

## PREPARATION

1. Sprinkle chicken with salt and pepper; place in slow cooker. Combine ginger, garlic, chicken broth, and syrup from pineapple; set aside. Cut pineapple slices into quarters. Arrange pineapple and sliced water chestnuts over chicken. Pour garlic ginger sauce over all. Cover and cook on HIGH 1 hour; reduce heat to low and cook an additional 3 to 5 hours or until chicken is tender. Add green onions. Dissolve cornstarch in soy sauce and vinegar then stir into crockpot.
2. Cover and cook on HIGH 10 to 15 minutes longer, or until slightly thickened.
3. Serve with hot cooked rice.

# Chicken with Grapes

### INGREDIENTS

- 4 to 6 boneless, skinless chicken breast halves • 1 tablespoon butter

- 2 tablespoons lemon juice • 1 tablespoon dry sherry or white wine • 8 to 12 ounces fresh mushrooms sliced • salt and pepper to taste • 1 tablespoon cornstarch mixed with 1 tablespoon water • 1 cup green seedless grapes

### PREPARATION

1. Place chicken, butter, lemon juice, sherry, mushrooms, and salt and pepper in the slow cooker/Crock Pot. Cover and cook on low for 6 to 8 hours. Stir in the cornstarch mixture and grapes during the last 45 minutes. (May be cooked on high 3 1/2 to 4 1/2 hours, adding grapes the last 20 minutes. Serve over rice.

2. Serves 4 to 6.

# Chicken With Honey

### INGREDIENTS

• 3 to 4 pounds chicken pieces • cup soy sauce • 1/2 cup water • honey

salt, pepper, and garlic powder • 1/2 cup green onion,

chopped 1/2 1/2 cup

### PREPARATION

1. Sprinkle chicken with salt, pepper, and a little garlic powder; place in slow cooker. Combine water, soy sauce, and chopped onion and pour over chicken. Cover and cook on LOW 3-4 hours or until chicken is render. Remove chicken from pot. Arrange on broiler pan and brush honey on chicken. Broil until golden brown, brushing with honey several times.

2. Serves 4.

# Chicken with Macaroni and Smoked Gouda Cheese

## INGREDIENTS

• 1 1/2 pounds chicken tenders, boneless • 2 small zucchini, halved and sliced 1/8-inch thick • 1 package chicken gravy mix (approx. 1 oz) • 2 tablespoons water • salt and pepper to taste • pinch of ground nutmeg, fresh if possible • 8 ounces smoked Gouda cheese, grated • 2 tablespoons evaporated milk or light cream • 1 large tomato, chopped • 4 cups cooked macaroni or small shell pasta

## PREPARATION

1. Cut chicken into 1-inch cubes; place in crockpot. Add zucchini, gravy mix, water, and seasoning. Cover and cook for 5 to 6 hours on low. Add smoked gouda cheese, milk or cream, and chopped tomato to the crockpot during the last 20 minutes, or while the macaroni is cooking. Stir in hot cooked macaroni.

2. Chicken recipe serves 4.

# Chicken With Noodles, Slow Cooker

### INGREDIENTS

• 2 teaspoons chicken bouillon granules or base • 1 tablespoon chopped fresh parsley • 3/4 teaspoon poultry seasoning • 1/3 cup. diced Canadian bacon or smoked ham • 2 to 3 carrots, thinly sliced • 2 ribs celery, thinly sliced • 1 small onion, thinly sliced • 1/4 cup. water • 1 broiler-fryer chicken (about 3 pounds), cut up • 1 (10 3/4 oz.) can condensed cheddar cheese soup • 1 tablespoon all purpose flour • 1 (16 oz.) pkg. wide egg noodles, cooked and drained • 2 tablespoons sliced pimento • 2 tablespoons grated Parmesan cheese

### PREPARATION

1. In a small bowl, combine chicken bouillon or base, chopped parsley, and poultry seasoning; set aside.
2. In slow cooker, layer Canadian bacon or ham, carrots, celery and onion. Add water.
3. Remove skin and excess fat from chicken; rinse and pat dry. Place half the chicken in slow cooker. Sprinkle with half of the reserved seasoning mixture. Top with remaining chicken and sprinkle with remaining seasoning mixture.
4. Stir soup and flour together and spoon over the chicken; do not stir.
5. Cover and cook on HIGH for 3 to 3 1/2 hours or on low for 6 to 8 hours, or

*until chicken is tender and juices from chicken run clear when cut along the bone and vegetables are tender.*
*6. Put hot cooked noodles in a shallow 2 to 2 1/2 quart broiler proof serving dish. Arrange chicken over the noodles. Stir soup mixture and vegetables in crockpot until blended. Spoon vegetables and some of the liquid over chicken. Sprinkle with sliced pimiento and Parmesan cheese.*

*7. Broil 4 to 6 inches from heat source for 5 to 8 minutes, or until lightly browned.*

*8. Garnish with parsley sprig if desired.*

*9. Alpine chicken recipe serves 4 to 6.*

# Chicken with Onions

### INGREDIENTS

*• 4 large onions, sliced thinly • 5 cloves garlic, minced • 1/4 cup lemon juice • 1 teaspoon salt • 1/4 teaspoon cayenne pepper (or more if you like) • 4 to 6 frozen boneless chicken breasts, no need to thaw • hot cooked rice*

### PREPARATION

*1. Put all ingredients except rice in Crock Pot. Mix well. Cook for 4 to 6 hours on LOW, or until chicken is cooked through and still tender.*
*2. Serve over rice.*

# Chicken With Parsley Dumplings

### *INGREDIENTS*

• 4 to 6 chicken breast halves, skin removed • 1 dash each salt, pepper, dried leaf thyme, ground marjoram and paprika • 1 large onion, sliced, divided • 2 leeks, sliced • 4 carrots, cut large chunks • 1 garlic clove, minced • 1 cup chicken broth • 1 tablespoon cornstarch • 1 can (10 3/4 ounces) condensed cream of chicken soup • 1/2 cup dry white wine

• Dumplings • 1 cup Bisquick • 8 tablespoons milk • 1 teaspoon dried parsley flakes • dash salt • dash pepper • dash paprika

### *PREPARATION*

1. Sprinkle salt, pepper, thyme, marjoram, and paprika on chicken. In bottom of crockpot, place half of the onion slices, leeks, and carrots. Arrange chicken on vegetables. Sprinkle minced garlic over the chicken then top with remaining onion slices. Dissolve 1 tablespoon cornstarch in 1 cup of chicken broth then combine with the cream of chicken soup and wine. Cook on HIGH for about 3 hours or on LOW for about 6 hours (If cooking on LOW, turn to HIGH when dumplings are added).

2. Chicken should be tender, but not dry.

3. Dumplings: Mix together 1 cup bisquick, about 8 tablespoon milk,

*parsley, salt, pepper, and paprika; form into balls and place on top of the chicken mixture the last 35 to 45 minutes of cooking.*
*4. Serves 4 to 6.*

# Chicken With Pearl Onions and Mushrooms

### *INGREDIENTS*

• 4 to 6 boneless chicken breast halves, cut in 1-inch chunks • 1 can (10 3/4 ounces) cream of chicken or cream of chicken and mushroom soup • 8 ounces sliced mushrooms • 1 bag (16 ounces) frozen pearl onions • salt and pepper, to taste • parsley, chopped, for garnish

### *PREPARATION*

1. Wash chicken and pat dry. Cut into chunks about 1/2 to 1-inch and put in a large bowl. Add the soup, mushrooms, and onions; stir to combine. Spray the slow cooker insert with cooking spray.
2. Spoon the chicken mixture into the crockpot and sprinkle with salt and pepper.
3. Cover and cook on LOW for 6 to 8 hours, stirring about halfway through the cooking time, if possible.
4. Garnish with fresh chopped parsley, if desired, and serve over hot cooked rice or with potatoes.
5. Serves 4 to 6.

# Chicken With Pineapple

### *INGREDIENTS*

• 1 to 1 1/2 pounds chicken tenders, cut in 1-inch pieces • 2/3 cup pineapple preserves • 1 tablespoon plus 1 teaspoon teriyaki sauce • 2 cloves garlic sliced thinly • 1 tablespoon dried minced onion (or 1 bunch fresh green onions, chopped) • 1 tablespoon lemon juice • 1/2 teaspoon ground ginger • dash cayenne, to taste • 1 package (10 oz) sugar snap peas, thawed

### *PREPARATION*

1. Place chicken pieces in slow cooker/Crock Pot.
2. Combine preserves, teriyaki sauce, garlic, onion, lemon juice, ginger, and

   cayenne; stir well. Spoon over chicken, toss to coat.
3. Cover and cook on low 6 to 7 hours. Add peas last 30 minutes.
4. Serves 4.

# Chicken-Rice Casserole

### *INGREDIENTS*

*• 4 to 6 large chicken breasts, boneless, skinned • 1 can cream of chicken soup • 1 can cream of celery soup • 1 can cream of mushroom soup*
*• 1/2 cup diced celery • 1 to 1 1/2 cups converted rice*

### *PREPARATION*

*1. In slow cooker, combine 3 cans of soup and rice. Place the chicken on top of the mixture, then add the diced celery. Cook for 3 hours on high or about 6 to 7 hours on low.*
*2. Makes 4 to 6 servings.*

# Chili Chicken

## INGREDIENTS

• 6 boneless chicken breast halves, cut in 1-inch pieces • 1 cup chopped onion • 1 cup chopped bell pepper • 2 garlic cloves • 2 tbsp. vegetable oil • 2 cans Mexican stewed tomatoes (approx. 15 ounces each) • 1 can chili beans • 2/3 cup picante sauce • 1 teaspoon. chili powder • 1 teaspoon. cumin • 1/2 teaspoon. salt

## PREPARATION

1. Saute chicken, onion, pepper, garlic in vegetable oil until vegetables are wilted. Transfer to slow cooker; add remaining ingredients. Cover and cook on LOW for 4 to 6 hours. Serve with rice.
2. Serves 4 to 6.

# Chinese-Style Chicken and Vegetables

## *INGREDIENTS*

• 1 to 1 1/2 pounds chicken breast tenders, boneless • 2 cups coarsely chopped cabbage • 1 medium onion, cut in large chunks • 1 medium red bell pepper, cut in large chunks • 1 packet Kikkoman Chicken Salad Seasoning • 1 tablespoon red wine vinegar • 2 teaspoons honey • 1 tablespoon soy sauce • 1 cup frozen mixed oriental vegetables • 2 tablespoons cornstarch • 1 tablespoon cold water

## *PREPARATION*

1. Cut chicken into 1 1/2-inch pieces. Place first 8 ingredients in slow cooker; mix well. Cover and cook on low for 5 to 7 hours. Stir cornstarch and cold water together; add with vegetables and cook for 30 to 45 minutes longer, until vegetables are tender.

2. Serves 4 to 6.

# Cornish Game Hens with Rice

### INGREDIENTS

• 2 Cornish game hens • 1/2 cup chicken broth • Salt and lemon pepper to taste • hot boiled rice

### PREPARATION

1. Place Cornish hens in the slow cooker (brown hens in a lightly greased skillet first, if desired). Add chicken broth. Sprinkle the hens with salt and lemon pepper. Cook on LOW setting for 7 to 9 hours. Remove hens and skim fat; thicken juices with a mixture of 1 1/2 tablespoons of cornstarch and 1 tablespoon cold water. Serve with hot cooked rice. Serves 2.

# Cornish Hens with Raisin Sauce

## INGREDIENTS

- 1 package (6 ounces) stuffing mix, prepared as directed
- 4 Cornish game hens
- salt and pepper
- .
- Raisin Sauce
- 1 jar (10 ounces) currant jelly
- 1/2 cup raisins
- 1/4 cup butter
- 1 tablespoon lemon juice
- 1/4 teaspoon allspice

## PREPARATION

1. Stuff hens with prepared stuffing; sprinkle with salt and pepper. Place trivet or crumpled piece of heavy-duty foil in slow cooker, to keep hens from sitting in juices. If you're using a deep and narrow crockpot, put Cornish hens in neck-side down. In a 1-quart saucepan combine jelly, raisins, butter, lemon juice and allspice. Cook over low heat, stirring, until hot and simmering. Brush some of the sauce on hens in the crockpot.
2. Keep remaining sauce in refrigerator until serving time. Cover and cook on LOW for 5 to 7 hours, basting once about an hour before done. Bring remaining sauce to a boil and spoon over hens at serving time.
3. Makes 4 servings.

# Country Captain Chicken Breasts

### INGREDIENTS

- 2 medium-size Granny Smith apples, cored and diced (unpeeled)
- 1/4 cup finely chopped onion
- 1 small green bell pepper, seeded and finely chopped
- 3 cloves garlic, minced
- 2 tablespoons raisins or currants
- to 3 teaspoons curry powder
- 1 teaspoon ground ginger
- 1/4 teaspoon ground red pepper, or to taste
- 1 can (about 14 1/2 oz.) diced tomatoes
- boneless chicken breast halves, skin removed
- 1/2 cup chicken broth
- cup long-grain converted white rice
- 1 pound medium to large shrimp, shelled and deveined, uncooked, optional
- 1/3 cup slivered almonds
- kosher salt
- Chopped parsley

### PREPARATION

1. In a 4-to 6-quart slow cooker, combine diced apples, onion, bell pepper, garlic, golden raisins or currants, curry powder, ginger, and ground red pepper; stir in tomatoes.
2. Arrange the chicken over the tomato mixture, overlapping pieces slightly. Pour chicken broth over the chicken breast halves. Cover and cook on LOW until chicken is very tender when pierced with a fork, about 4 to 6 hours.
3. Remove chicken to a warm plate, cover lightly, and keep warm in a 200° F oven or warming drawer.

4. Stir the rice into cooking liquid. Increase temperature to high; cover and cook, stirring once or twice, until rice is almost tender, about 35 minutes. Stir in shrimp, if using; cover and cook for about 15 minutes longer, until shrimp are opaque in center; cut to test.

5. Meanwhile, toast almonds in a small nonstick frying pan over medium heat until golden brown, stirring occasionally. Set aside.

6. To serve the dish, season rice mixture to taste with salt. Mound in a warm serving dish; arrange chicken on top. Sprinkle with parsley and almonds.

# Country Chicken and Mushrooms

### INGREDIENTS

*• 1 jar country gravy • 4 to 6 chicken breasts • 8 ounces sliced mushrooms • salt and pepper to taste*

### PREPARATION

*1. Combine all ingredients; cover and cook on low for 6 to 7 hours. Serve with rice or noodles.*
*2. Serves 4 to 6.*

# Country Club Chicken

### INGREDIENTS

• 5 apples, peeled, cored & chopped • 6 to 8 green onions, with green, sliced • 1 lb chicken thighs, deboned, skinned, all fat removed, cut into 2-inch cubes • 6 to 8 ounces sliced Swiss cheese • 1 can (10 1/2 ounces) cream of chicken soup, well blended with 1/4 cup milk • 1 box (6 ounces) Pepperidge Farm Stuffing with Apples and Raisins, or use your favorite stuffing mix
• 1/4 cup melted butter • 3/4 cup apple juice

### PREPARATION

1. Layer ingredients in 3-1/2 to 5-quart slow cooker in same order as above. Pour soup mixture over cheese layer, butter over stuffing and finally drizzle with the apple juice, making sure that liquid moistens all of the bread.

2. Cover and cook on HIGH for 1 hour and on LOW for another 4 to 5 hours.

3. Rose-Marie's Note: 4. We ate it without anything but since it makes a

wonderful sauce and the stuffing sort of disappears into the dish, I recommend serving it with plain rice.

# Cranberry Chicken

### INGREDIENTS

- 4 to 6 boneless chicken breast halves, skin removed • 1 can whole cranberry sauce • 2/3 cup chili sauce • 2 tablespoons cider vinegar • 2 tablespoons brown sugar • 1 package dry (Lipton) golden onion soup mix

### PREPARATION

1. Place chicken breasts in the slow cooker/Crock Pot. Combine remaining ingredients; add to the slow cooker/Crock Pot, coating chicken well. Cover and cook on low 6 to 8 hours.
2. Serves 4 to 6.

# Cranberry Chicken II

## *INGREDIENTS*

• 2 pounds boneless chicken breasts, skin removed • 1/2 cup chopped onion • 2 teaspoons vegetable oil • 2 teaspoons salt • 1/2 teaspoon ground cinnamon • 1/4 teaspoon ground ginger • 1/8 teaspoon ground nutmeg • dash ground allspice • 1 cup orange juice • 2 teaspoons finely grated orange peel • 2 cups fresh or frozen cranberries • 1/4 cup brown sugar

## *PREPARATION*

1. Brown chicken pieces and onion in oil; sprinkle with salt.
2. Add browned chicken, onions and other ingredients to crock pot.
3. Cover and cook on LOW 5 1/2 to 7 hours.
4. If desired, thicken juices near the end of cooking time with a mixture of

about 2 tablespoons cornstarch combined with 2 tablespoons cold water.

# Cream Cheese Chicken

### INGREDIENTS

• 3 to 3 1/2 pounds chicken parts • 2 tablespoons melted butter • salt and pepper, to taste • 2 tablespoons dry Italian salad dressing • 1 can (10 3/4 ounces) cream of mushroom soup • 8 ounces cream cheese, cut into cubes • 1/2 cup dry white wine • 1 tablespoon chopped onion

### PREPARATION

1. Brush chicken with butter and sprinkle with salt and pepper. Place in a slow cooked and sprinkle dry dressing mix over all.
2. Cover and cook on low for 6 to 7 hours, or until the chicken is tender and cooked through.
3. About 45 minutes before done, mix soup, cream cheese, wine, and onion in a small saucepan. Cook until bubbly and smooth.
4. Pour over the chicken and cover and cook 30 to 45 minutes longer.
5. Serve chicken with sauce.
6. Serves 4 to 6.

# Creamy Chicken and Artichokes

### INGREDIENTS

• 2 to 3 cups cooked, cubed chicken • 2 cups frozen artichoke quarters or 1 can (about 15 ounces), drained • 2 ounces chopped pimiento, drained • 1 jar (16 ounces) Alfredo sauce • 1 teaspoon chicken base or bouillon • 1/2 teaspoon dried basil • 1/2 teaspoon garlic granules or powder • 1 teaspoon dried parsley, optional • salt and pepper to taste • 8 ounces spaghetti, cooked and drained, optional

### PREPARATION

1. I poach about a pound of chicken tenders in a little lemon and garlic seasoned water, but you can use cooked chicken breasts or leftover chicken. Combine all ingredients in the crockpot; cover and cook on low for 4 to 6 hours. Stir in hot cooked pasta or use as a sauce for rice or pasta. This slow cooker chicken and artichokes recipe serves 4 to 6.

# Creamy Italian Chicken

### INGREDIENTS

• 4 boneless skinless chicken breast halves • 1 envelope Italian salad dressing mix • 1/3 cup water • 1 package (8 ozs.) cream cheese, softened • 1 can (10 3/4 ozs.) condensed cream of chicken soup, undiluted • 1 can (4 ozs.) mushroom stems and pieces, drained • Hot cooked rice or noodles

### PREPARATION

1. Place the chicken breast halves in a slow cooker. Combine salad dressing mix and water; pour over chicken. Cover and cook on LOW for 3 hours. In a small mixing bowl, whisk together cream cheese and soup until blended. Stir in mushrooms. Pour cream cheese mixture over chicken. Cook 1 to 3 hours longer or until chicken juices run clear. Serve Italian chicken with rice or hot cooked noodles.

2. Serves 4.

# Creole Chicken

### *INGREDIENTS*

• 1 frying chicken, cut up, about 3 pounds chicken pieces • 1 green bell pepper, chopped • 6 green onions, about 1 bunch, chopped • 1 can (14.5 ounces) tomatoes, undrained, cut up • 1 can (6 ounces) tomato paste • 4 ounces cooked diced ham • 1 teaspoon salt • several drops of bottled hot pepper sauce, such as Tabasco • 1/2 pound sliced smoked sausage, andouille, kielbasa, etc.

• 3 cups cooked rice

### *PREPARATION*

1. In slow cooker, combine the chicken, pepper, onions, tomatoes, tomato paste, ham, salt, and pepper sauce.
2. Cover and cook on low for 6 hours. Turn control to high and add sausage and cooked rice. Cover and cook on high for 20 minutes longer.

# Creole Chicken With Sausage

### INGREDIENTS

*1 1/2 pounds boneless chicken thighs, cut into chunks • 12 ounces smoked andouille sausage, cut in 1-to 2-inch lengths • 1 cup chopped onions*

*3/4 cup chicken broth or water •*

*1 can (6 ounces) tomato paste •*

*dash cayenne pepper, to taste •
pepper, to taste • hot cooked white or brown rice or cooked drained spaghetti*

### PREPARATION

1. In a slow cooker, combine the chicken thigh pieces, andouille sausage pieces, chopped onions, broth or water, tomatoes (with their juices), tomato paste, Creole seasoning, and cayenne pepper.
2. Cover and cook the chicken and sausage mixture on LOW for 6 to 7 hours. Add the chopped green bell pepper about an hour before the dish is done. Taste and add salt and pepper, as needed.

3. Serve this flavorful chicken and sausage dish over hot boiled rice, or serve it with spaghetti or angel hair pasta.
4. Serves 6.

*1 can (14.5 ounces) diced tomatoes
2 teaspoons Cajun or Creole seasoning*

*1 green bell pepper, chopped • salt and*

# Crock Pot Chicken and Artichokes

### INGREDIENTS

- 3 pounds chicken pieces, broiler-fryer, cut up • salt, to taste • 1/2 teaspoon pepper • 1/2 teaspoon paprika • 1 tablespoon butter • 2 jars marinated artichoke, hearts; reserve marinade • 1 can (4 ounces) mushrooms, drained • 2 tablespoons quick-cooking tapioca • 1/2 cup chicken broth

- 3 tablespoons dry sherry or more chicken broth • 1/2 teaspoon dried tarragon

### PREPARATION

1. Wash chicken and pat dry. Season chicken with salt, pepper, and paprika. In a large skillet over medium heat, brown chicken in butter and the reserved marinade from artichokes.
2. Place mushrooms and artichoke hearts in bottom of slow cooker. Sprinkle with tapioca. Add the browned chicken pieces. Pour in chicken broth and sherry. Add tarragon. Cover and cook on LOW for 7 to 8 hours, or cook on HIGH for 3 1/2 to 4 1/2 hours.

3. Serves 4.

# Crock Pot Chicken And Dressing

### *INGREDIENTS*

- 4 boneless chicken breast halves, without skin+
- salt and freshly ground black pepper, to taste • 4 slices swiss cheese
- 1 can (10 3/4 ounces) condensed cream of chicken soup • 1 can (10 3/4 ounces) condensed cream of mushroom soup or cream of celery • 1 cup chicken broth • 1/4 cup milk • 3 cups herb seasoned stuffing crumbs
- 1/2 cup melted butter

### *PREPARATION*

1. Season chicken breasts with salt and pepper and place them in the slow cooker. Pour chicken broth over chicken breasts. Put one slice of Swiss cheese on each breast.
2. Combine both cans of soup and the milk in a bowl; blend well. Pour the soup mixture over the chicken. Sprinkle stuffing mix over all. Drizzle melted butter over the stuffing layer.
3. Cover and cook on low for 5 to 7 hours.//
4. **Note: Chicken breasts are very lean and become dry when overcooked.**

5. Depending on your slow cooker, the chicken might be done perfectly in 4 hours or less. For the longer cooking time, try the recipe with boneless chicken thighs.

# Crock Pot Chicken Enchilada Hot Dish

### INGREDIENTS

- 9 corn tortillas, 6-inch
- 1 can (12 to 16 ounces) whole kernel corn with peppers, drained
- 2 to 3 cups cooked diced chicken
- 1 teaspoon chili powder
- 1/4 teaspoon ground black pepper
- 1/2 teaspoon salt, or to taste
- 1 can (4 ounces) chopped green chile peppers, mild
- 2 cups shredded Mexican blend cheese or mild Cheddar cheese
- 2 cans (10 ounces each) enchilada sauce
- 1 can (15 ounces) black beans, rinsed and drained
- guacamole and sour cream

### PREPARATION

1. Spray slow cooker with nonstick cooking spray.
2. Place 3 tortillas in bottom of slow cooker.
3. Top tortillas with the corn, half of the chicken, about half of the seasonings, and half of the chile peppers.
4. Sprinkle with half of the shredded cheese and pour about 3/4 cup of enchilada sauce over the cheese.
5. Repeat with 3 more tortillas, the black beans, remaining chicken, seasonings, chile peppers, and cheese.
6. Top with remaining tortillas and enchilada sauce.
7. Cover and cook on LOW setting for 5 to 6 hours.

3. Serve with guacamole and sour cream.

4. Serves 6 to 8.

# Crock Pot Chicken Enchiladas

### INGREDIENTS

- *1 large can (19 ounces) enchilada sauce • 6 boneless chicken breast halves • 2 cans cream of chicken soup • 1 small can sliced black olives*
- *1/2 cup chopped onion • 1 can (4 ounces) chopped mild chile peppers*
- *16 to 20 corn tortillas • 16 ounces shredded sharp Cheddar cheese*

### PREPARATION

*1. Cook chicken and shred. Mix soup, olives, chile peppers, and onions. Cut tortillas in wedges. Layer Crock Pot with sauce, tortillas, soup mix, chicken and cheese all the way to top, ending with cheese on top. Cover and cook on LOW for 5 to 7 hours.*

*2. Serves 8 to 10*

# Crock Pot Chicken Tortillas

### INGREDIENTS

• 4 cups cooked chicken shredded or cut into bite-size pieces • 1 can cream of chicken soup • 1/2 c. green chile salsa • 2 tbsp. quick cooking tapioca
• 1 med. onion, chopped • 1 1/2 c. shredded cheese • 12 to 15 corn tortillas • Black olives • 1 tomato, chopped • 2 tablespoons chopped green onion • sour cream for garnish

### PREPARATION

1. Combine chicken with soup, chile salsa, and tapioca. Line bottom of Crock Pot with 3 corn tortillas, torn into bite size pieces. Add 1/3 of the chicken mixture. Sprinkle with 1/3 of the onion and 1/3 of the grated cheese. Repeat layers of tortillas topped with chicken mixture, onions and cheese. Cover and cook on low 6 to 8 hours or high for 3 hours. Garnish with sliced black olives, chopped tomatoes, green onion, and sour cream, if desired.

# Crockpot Cassoulet

### INGREDIENTS

- 1 pound dry navy beans, rinsed • 4 cups water • 4 boneless chicken breast halves without skin, cut in 1-inch pieces • 8 ounces cooked ham, cut in 1-inch pieces • 3 large carrots, thinly sliced • 1 cup chopped onion • 1/2 cup sliced celery • 1/4 cup firmly packed brown sugar • 1/2 teaspoon salt

- 1/4 teaspoon dry mustard • 1/4 teaspoon pepper • 1 can (8 ounces) tomato sauce • 2 tablespoons molasses

### PREPARATION

2. In Dutch oven or large kettle, soak beans overnight in 4 cups water.

3. Cover and simmer beans over low heat for about 1 1/2 hours, until tender,

   adding a little more water as necessary.
4. Put the beans and liquid in the crockpot. Add remaining ingredients; mix well.

5. Cover and cook on LOW for 7 to 9 hours, until vegetables are tender.

6. Serves 6 to 8.

# Crockpot Chicken and Herb Dumplings

## *INGREDIENTS*

• 3 pounds chicken pieces, skin removed • salt and pepper • 1/4 cup chopped onions • 10 small white onions • 2 cloves garlic, minced • 1/4 teaspoon ground marjoram • 1/2 teaspoon dried leaf thyme, crumbled • 1 bay leaf • 1/2 cup dry white wine • 1 cup dairy sour cream • 1 cup biscuit mix • 1 tablespoon chopped parsley • 6 tablespoons milk

## *PREPARATION*

1. Sprinkle chicken with salt and pepper, place in slow cooker or crockpot. Put all onions into pot. Add garlic, marjoram, thyme, bay leaf and wine. Cover and cook on low 5 to 6 hours. Remove bay leaf. Stir in sour cream. Increase heat to high and combine biscuit mix with parsley. Stir milk into biscuit mix until well moistened. Drop dumplings from teaspoon around edge of pot. Cover and continue to cook on high for 30 minutes longer, until dumplings are cooked.

# Crockpot Chicken Barbecue

## *INGREDIENTS*

• 2 boneless, skinless chicken breasts • 1 1/2 cups tomato ketchup • 3 tablespoons brown sugar • 1 tablespoon Worcestershire sauce • 1 tablespoon soy sauce • 1 tablespoon cider vinegar • 1 teaspoon ground red hot pepper flakes, or to taste • 1/2 teaspoon garlic powder

## *PREPARATION*

1. Combine all ingredients for the sauce in the slow cooker. Add the chicken; turn to coat thoroughly with the sauce.
2. Cook on high 3 to 4 hours, or until chicken is fully cooked. Shred or chop chicken, and return it to the sauce in the pot. Mix well so all the pieces are coated.

3. You can keep the slow cooker on low to keep the chicken warm for serving on hard rolls.
4. Delicious!

# Crockpot Chicken Chili

## *INGREDIENTS*

• 2 cups great northern dried beans, soaked overnight • 3 cups boiling water • 1 cup chopped onion • 2 garlic cloves, minced • 2 to 3 canned jalapeno peppers, chopped (pickled is fine) • 1 tablespoon ground cumin • 1 teaspoon chili powder • 1 to 1 1/2 pounds boneless chicken breasts, cut into 1-inch pieces • 2 small zucchini or summer squash, cubed • 1 can (12 to 15 ounces) whole kernel corn, drained • 1/2 cup sour cream • 2 1/4 teaspoons salt • 1 tablespoon lime juice • 1/4 cup chopped fresh cilantro, and some for garnish, if desired • 1 tomato, chopped, for garnish, or halved cherry tomatoes • sour cream for garnish

## *PREPARATION*

1. Combine beans and boiling water in slow-cooker. Let stand while preparing other ingredients. Add chopped onion, minced garlic, jalapeno pepper, cumin and chili powder to the crockpot. Place chicken on top. Add cubed squash to the pot. Cover and cook on low heat for 7 to 8 hours or until beans are tender. Stir in corn, sour cream, salt, lime juice and chopped cilantro. Spoon into bowls. Garnish with a spoonful of sour cream, chopped tomato and chopped fresh cilantro, if desired.

# Crockpot Chicken Chow Mein

### INGREDIENTS

- 1 1/2 pounds boneless chicken breasts, cut into 1-inch chunks
- 1 tablespoon vegetable oil • 1 1/2 cups chopped celery • 1 1/2 cups chopped

carrots •
sauce •
ginger •

ounces) ounces bean sprouts, drained • 1 can (8 ounces) sliced water chestnuts, drained • 1/4 cup cornstarch • 1/3 cup water

6 green onions, chopped • 1 cup chicken broth • 1/3 cup soy 1/4 teaspoon ground red pepper, or to taste • 1/2 teaspoon ground

1 clove garlic, finely minced • 1 can (approximately 12 to 15

### PREPARATION

1. In a large skillet, brown chicken pieces. Put browned chicken in the slow cooker. Add remaining ingredients except cornstarch and water. Stir. Cover and cook on LOW for 6 to 8 hours. Turn the slow cooker to HIGH . Mix cornstarch and water in a small bowl, stirring until dissolved and smooth. Stir into the slow cooker liquids. Keeping cover slightly ajar to allow steam to escape, cook until thickened, about 20 to 30 minutes.

2. Serve with rice or chow mein noodles. May be doubled for 5 qt. slow cooker/Crock Pots.

# Crockpot Chicken Cordon Bleu

## *INGREDIENTS*

*• 4-6 chicken breasts (pounded out thin) • 4-6 pieces of ham • 4-6 slices of Swiss or mozzarella cheese • 1 can cream of mushroom soup (can use any cream soup) • 1/4 cup milk*

## *PREPARATION*

*1. Put ham and cheese on chicken. Roll up and secure with a toothpick. Place chicken in the slow cooker/Crock Pot so it looks like a triangle /_ \ Layer the rest on top. Mix soup with the milk; pour over top of chicken. Cover and cook on low for 4 hours or until chicken is no longer pink. Serve over noodles with the sauce it makes.*

*2. Teresa's Note: Its the best recipe I've tried so far, very flavorful.*

# Crockpot Chicken Dinner

### INGREDIENTS

• 4 boneless chicken breast halves • 2 pounds small white potatoes, peeled and cut in 1-inch cubes • onion, cut in thin wedges • fresh chopped parsley • tablespoons melted butter, divided • 2 tablespoons Spanish smoked paprika • 1 tablespoon lemon juice • 1 teaspoon Worcestershire sauce • 1 tablespoon honey • Dash salt • Dash cumin

### PREPARATION

1. Wash chicken and pat dry. Combine potatoes, carrots, and onion wedges in a 4-to 6-quart slow cooker with parsley, 1 teaspoon salt, 1/4 teaspoon pepper, and 2 tablespoons of the melted butter; toss.

2. Combine the remaining 2 tablespoons of butter with the smoked paprika, lemon juice, Worcestershire sauce, honey, and dash of salt and dash of cumin. Rub chicken breasts with the paprika mixture; arrange on vegetables.

3. Cover and cook on HIGH for 3 1/2 to 4 1/2 hours, or on LOW for 7 to 9 hours, until chicken is cooked through and vegetables are tender.

4. Serves 4.

# Crockpot Chicken Drumsticks

### INGREDIENTS

• 12 to 16 chicken drumsticks, skin removed • 1 cup maple syrup • 1/2 cup soy sauce • 1 can (14 ounces) whole berry cranberry sauce • 1 teaspoon Dijon mustard • 1 tablespoon cornstarch • 1 tablespoon cold water • sliced green onions or fresh chopped cilantro, optional

### PREPARATION

1. If you choose to leave the skin on the drumsticks, put the chicken in a large saucepan, cover with water, and bring to a boil over high heat. Boil for about 5 minutes. Parboiling will remove some of the excess fat from the skin.

2. Remove the chicken, pat dry, and place the drumsticks in the slow cooker.

3. In a bowl combine the maple syrup, soy sauce, cranberry sauce, and

   mustard. Pour over the drumsticks.

4. Cover and cook for 6 to 7 hours on LOW or about 3 hours on HIGH. The chicken should be very tender, but not completely falling apart.

5. Remove the chicken drumsticks to a platter and keep warm.

6. Combine the cornstarch and cold water in a cup or small bowl. Stir until

smooth.

7. Increase the slow cooker temperature to high and stir in the cornstarch mixture. Cook for about 10 minutes, until thickened.

8. Or transfer the liquids to a saucepan and bring to a boil. Stir in the cornstarch mixture and cook, stirring for a minute or two until the sauce has thickened.

9. Serve garnished with sliced green onions or chopped cilantro if desired. **10. Variations** 11. Use bone-in chicken thighs or in place of the drumsticks. Remove the skin before cooking.

12. Use 6 to 8 whole, skinless chicken legs instead of drumsticks.

# Crockpot Chicken Fricassee Recipe

### INGREDIENTS

- 1 can condensed cream of chicken soup, reduced fat or Healthy Request
- 1/4 cup water • 1/2 cup chopped onions • 1 teaspoon ground paprika
- 1 teaspoon lemon juice • 1 teaspoon dried rosemary, crushed • 1

teaspoon thyme •
teaspoon pepper •
stick cooking spray •
1/2 cups flour • 2 tsp. baking powder • 3/4 tsp. salt • 3 tablespoons fresh chopped chives or parsley • 3/4 cup skim milk

1 teaspoon parsley flakes • 1 teaspoon salt • 1/4
4 boneless chicken breast halves, without skin • non-

Chive Dumplings • 3 tablespoons shortening • 1

### PREPARATION

1. Spray slow cooker with non-stick cooking spray. Place chicken in slow cooker.
2. Combine soup, water, onions, paprika, lemon juice,

rosemary, thyme, parsley, 1 teaspoon salt, and pepper; pour over chicken. Cover and cook on LOW for 6 to 7 hours. One hour before serving time, prepare the dumplings, below.

3. Dumplings: 4. With pastry blender or forks, work dry ingredients and shortening together until the mixture resembles coarse meal.

5. Add chives or parsley and milk; mix just until well combined. With teaspoon, drop onto hot chicken and gravy. Cover and continue cooking on HIGH for about 25 minutes longer, until dumplings are cooked. Serve with mashed potatoes or noodles, along with vegetables or a salad.

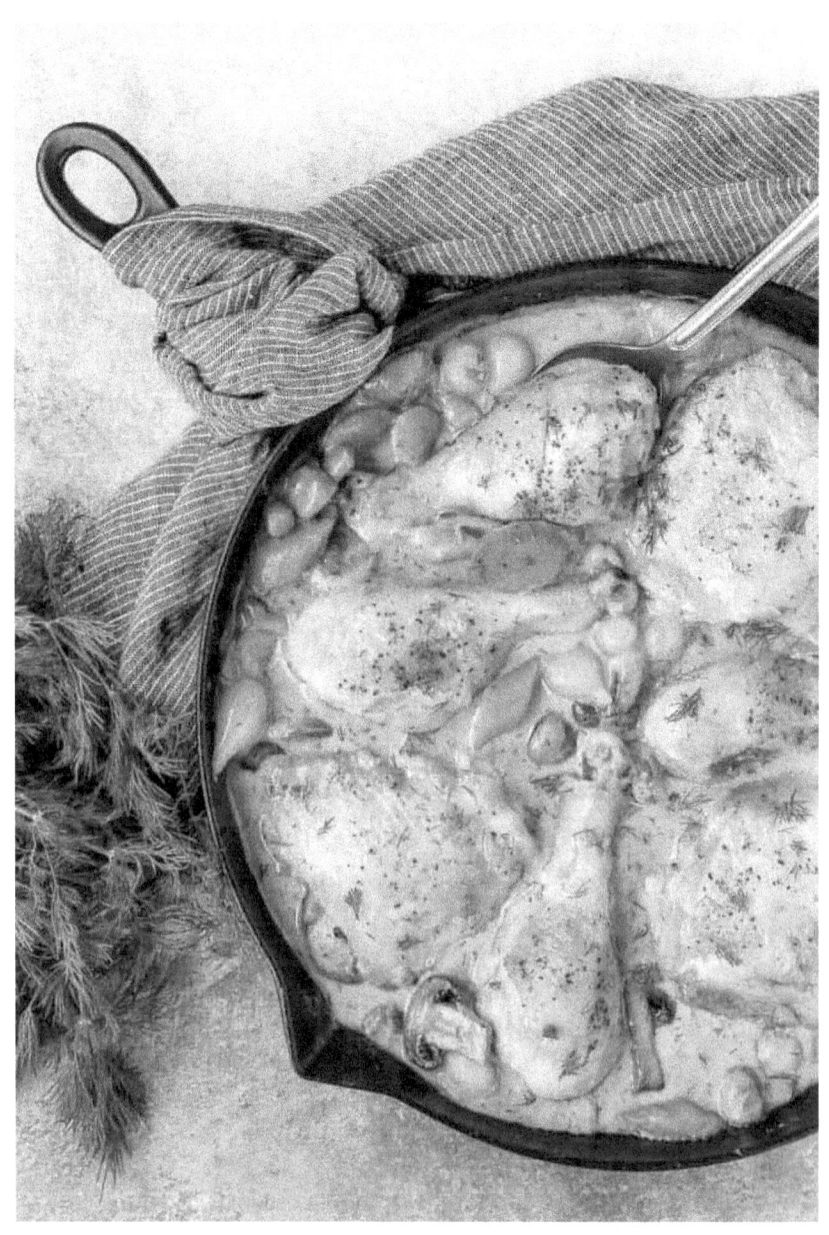

# Crockpot Chicken Reuben Casserole

### INGREDIENTS

• 2 bags (16 ounces each) sauerkraut, rinsed and drained • 1 cup light or low calorie Russian salad dressing, divided • 6 boneless chicken breast halves, without skin • 1 tablespoon prepared mustard • 4 to 6 slices Swiss cheese • fresh parsley, for garnish, optional

### PREPARATION

1. Place half the sauerkraut in a 3 1/2 quart electric slow cooker. Drizzle on about 1/3 cup of the dressing. Top with 3 chicken breast halves and spread the mustard over the chicken. Top with the remaining sauerkraut and chicken breasts. Drizzle another 1/3 cup dressing over the casserole. Refrigerate the remaining dressing until serving them. Cover and cook on the low heat setting about 3 1/2 to 4 hours, or until the chicken is white throughout and tender.

2. To serve, spoon the casserole onto 6 plates. Top each with a slice of cheese and drizzle with a few teaspoons of the Russian dressing. Serve immediately, garnished with fresh parsley, if desired.

3. Serves 6.

# Crockpot Chicken With Artichokes

### INGREDIENTS

- 1 1/2 to 2 pounds boneless chicken breast halves, skin removed
- 8 ounces sliced fresh mushrooms
- 1 can (14.5 ounces) diced tomatoes
- 1 package frozen artichokes, 8 to 12 ounces
- 1 cup chicken broth
- 1/2 cup chopped onion
- 1 can (3 to 4 ounces) sliced ripe olives
- 1/4 cup dry white wine or chicken broth
- 3 tablespoons quick-cooking tapioca
- 2 teaspoons curry powder, or to taste
- 3/4 teaspoon dried thyme, crushed
- 1/4 teaspoon salt
- 1/4 teaspoon pepper
- 4 cups hot cooked rice

### PREPARATION

1. Rinse chicken; pat dry and set aside. In a 3 1/2 to 5-quart slow cooker combine the mushrooms, tomatoes, artichoke hearts, chicken broth, chopped onion, sliced olives, and wine. Stir in tapioca, curry powder, thyme, salt, and pepper. Add chicken to crockpot; spoon some of the tomato mixture over chicken.

2. Cover and cook on LOW for 7 to 8 hours or on HIGH for 3 1/2 to 4 hours. Serve with hot cooked rice.

3. Makes 6 to 8 servings.

# Crockpot Chicken with Dijon Mustard

### INGREDIENTS

- 4 to 6 boneless chicken breast halves • 2 tablespoons Dijon mustard
- 1 can 98% fat-free cream of mushroom soup • 2 teaspoons cornstarch
- dash black pepper

### PREPARATION

1. Place the chicken breast halves in the slow cooker insert.
2. Combine remaining ingredients and spoon over the chicken.
3. Cover and cook on low 6 to 8 hours.

# Crockpot Chicken With Tomatoes

### INGREDIENTS

• 4 to 6 chicken breast halves • 2 green bell peppers, sliced • 1 can chopped stewed tomatoes • 1/2 small bottle Italian dressing (low-fat if desired)

### PREPARATION

1. Place chicken breasts, green bell peppers, stewed tomatoes and Italian dressing in the slow cooker or crockpot and cook all day (6 to 8 hours) on low. 2. This recipe for chicken with stewed tomatoes shared by Myron in Florida

# Crockpot Cola Chicken

### INGREDIENTS

• 1 whole chicken, about 3 pounds • 1 cup ketchup • 1 large onion, thinly sliced • 1 cup cola, Coke, Pepsi, Dr. Pepper, etc.

### PREPARATION

1. Wash and pat chicken dry. Salt and pepper to taste. Put chicken in Crock Pot with the onions on top. Add cola and ketchup and cook on LOW 6 to 8 hours. Enjoy!
2. Posted by Molly

# Crockpot Creole Chicken

### INGREDIENTS

- 1 pound boneless chicken thighs, skin removed, cut into 1-inch pieces • 1 can (14.5 ounces) tomatoes with juice • 1 1/2 cups chicken broth • 8 ounces fully cooked smoked sausage, sliced • 1/2 to 1 cup diced cooked ham
- 1 cup chopped onion • 1 can (6 ounces) tomato paste • 1/4 cup water
- 1 1/2 teaspoons Creole seasoning • a few dashes of Tabasco sauce or other hot pepper sauce • 2 cups instant rice, uncooked•
- 1 cup chopped green bell pepper

### PREPARATION

1. Combine chicken, tomatoes, broth, sausage, ham, onion, tomato paste, water, seasoning, and Tabasco sauce in the slow cooker. Cover and cook on LOW for 5 to 6 hours.
2. Add rice• and green pepper to crockpot and cook for 10 minutes longer, or until rice is tender and most of the liquid is absorbed.
3. If desired, cook 1 1/2 cups of regular long grain rice and serve along with the chicken mixture.
4. Serves 6.

# Crockpot Herb Chicken With Stuffing

## INGREDIENTS

- 1 can (10 1/2 ounces) cream of chicken with herbs soup
- 1 can (10 1/2 ounces) cream of celery or cream of chicken soup
- 1/2 cup dry white wine or chicken broth
- 1 teaspoon dried parsley flakes
- 1 teaspoon dried leaf thyme, crumbled
- 1/2 teaspoon salt
- Dash black pepper
- 2 to 2 1/2 cups seasoned stuffing crumbs, about 6 ounces, divided
- 4 tablespoons butter, divided
- 6 to 8 boneless chicken breast halves, without skin

## PREPARATION

1.
2. Combine the soups, wine or broth, parsley, thyme, salt, and pepper.
3. Wash chicken and pat dry.
4. Lightly grease a 5 to 7-quart slow cooker insert.

5. Sprinkle about 1/2 cup of the stuffing crumbs over the bottom of the cooker and drizzle with about 1 tablespoon of the butter.

6. Top with half of the chicken, then half of the remaining stuffing crumbs. Drizzle with half of the remaining butter and spoon half of the soup mixture over that.

7. Repeat with remaining chicken, stuffing crumbs, butter, and soup mixture.

8. Cover and cook on LOW for 5 to 7 hours, or until chicken is cooked through. Serves 6 to 8.

# Crockpot Italian-Style Chicken

### INGREDIENTS

- 4 pounds chicken pieces • 3 tablespoons olive oil • 2 onions, sliced

- 1 teaspoon salt • 1/2 teaspoon fresh ground pepper • 2 celery ribs, cut in small chunks • 2 cups diced potatoes • 1 can (14.5 ounces) diced tomatoes, undrained • 1 teaspoon dried leaf oregano • 1 tablespoon dried parsley flakes • 1 cup frozen peas, thawed

### PREPARATION

1. Brown the chicken parts in hot oil. Add salt, pepper and onions and cook for another 5 minutes. Put celery and potatoes in the bottom of the slow cooker and top with browned chicken, onions, and tomatoes with juice, oregano, and parsley. Cover and cook on low for 6 to 8 hours. Add peas the last 30 minutes. 2. Serves 6.

# Crock Pot Lima Beans with Chicken

## INGREDIENTS

• 3 to 4 pounds chicken pieces • salt and pepper • 1 tablespoon vegetable oil • 2 large potatoes, cut in 1-inch cubes • 1 package frozen lima beans, thawed • 1 cup chicken broth • 1/4 teaspoon dried leaf thyme, crumbled

## PREPARATION

1. Season chicken with salt and pepper. Heat oil and butter in large skillet; fry chicken until browned on both sides. Place chicken in crockpot with remaining ingredients. Cover and cook on low for 4 to 6 hours, until chicken is tender.

2. Serves 4.

# Crockpot Pasta and Cheese Delight

### INGREDIENTS

- 1 jar Alfredo Sauce • 1 can Healthy Request Cream of Mushroom Soup

- 1 (7 oz) can white tuna or chicken, drained, or use leftover cooked chicken or meat • 1/4 teaspoon curry powder • 1 to 1 1/2 cups frozen mixed vegetables • 1 1/2 cups shredded Swiss cheese • 4 cups cooked pasta (macaroni, bow ties, shells)

### PREPARATION

1. Combine first 5 ingredients; cover and cook for 4 to 5 hours on LOW. Add Swiss cheese to the mixture during the last hour. Cook pasta according to package directions; drain and add to slow cooker. This would be just as good with cooked or canned chicken, leftover ham or just add extra veggies!

2. Serves 4.

# Debbie's Crockpot Chicken and Stuffing

## INGREDIENTS

• 1 package herb-seasoned stuffing mix, prepared • 4 to 6 boneless chicken breast halves or boneless thighs, without skin•

• 1 can (10 3/4 ounces) condensed cream of chicken soup, undiluted • 1 can (3 to 4 ounces or more) sliced mushrooms, drained

## PREPARATION

1. Butter the bottom and sides of the slow cooker crockery insert.

2. Prepare the packaged (or homemade) stuffing mix with butter and liquid as

   directed on package.

3. Layer the prepared stuffing in the bottom of the greased slow cooker.

4. Place the chicken pieces on top of the stuffing mixture. The chicken can

overlap some, but try to arrange with as little overlap as possible. If there is room, you could use more chicken.

5. Spoon the condensed cream of chicken soup over the chicken. You may also use cream of mushroom, or cream of celery, whatever you like. Top with the mushrooms. Be sure to stir the mushrooms around a little so they are coated with the soup.

6. Cover and cook on low for 5 to 7 hours.

7. •Chicken breasts tend to become dry over a long period of cooking, so

check them early. Thighs are fattier than the chicken breasts, so they can be cooked for a longer period of time.

# Diana's Chicken a la King

### INGREDIENTS

• 1 1/2 to 2 pounds boneless chicken tenders • 1 to 1 1/2 cup matchstick- cut carrots • 1 bunch green onions (scallions) sliced in 1/2-inch pieces • 1 jar Kraft pimiento or pimiento & olive process cheese spread (5oz) • 1 can 98% fat-free cream of chicken soup • 2 tablespoons dry sherry (optional)

• salt and pepper to taste

### PREPARATION

1. Put all ingredients in the slow cooker/Crock Pot (3 1/2-quart or larger) in the order given; stir to combine. Cover and cook on low for 7 to 9 hours. Serve over rice, toast, or biscuits.

2. Serves 6 to 8.

# Dilled Chicken with Veggies

### INGREDIENTS

*• 1 to 1 1/2 pounds chicken tenders, cut in 1-inch pieces • 1 tablespoon dried minced onion (or small onion, chopped) • 1 can regular or 98% fat reduced cream of mushroom soup • 1 packet (1oz) mushroom gravy mix (chicken or country gravy may be substituted) • 1 cup carrots • 1/2 to 1 teaspoon dill weed • seasoned salt and pepper to taste • 1 cup frozen peas*

### *PREPARATION*

1. Combine first 7 ingredients in the slow cooker/Crock Pot; cover and cook on low for 6 to 8 hours. Add frozen peas during the last 30 to 45 minutes. Serve with rice or mashed potatoes.
2. Serves 4.

# Don's Sweet and Sour Chicken

### INGREDIENTS

- 2 to 4 skinless chicken breasts • 1 large onion roughly chopped • 2 bell peppers roughly chopped (one green, one red) • 1 cup of broccoli florettes • 1/2 cup of carrot chunks • 1 large can of chunk pineapple (drain and SAVE the juice) • 1/4-1/2 cup of brown sugar(can use reg. sugar)

- Water/wine/white grape juice/orange juice etc. as needed for extra liquid

- 1 Tablespoon of cornstarch for every cup of liquid you end up with • hot sauce to taste, optional • salt and pepper to taste, optional • cinnamon, optional • allspice, optional • cloves, optional • curry powder, optional

### PREPARATION

1. Put chicken breasts in slow cooker or crockpot. Add the onion, peppers, broccoli, and carrots Whisk together until blended well, no lumps in sugar, liquids, spices, and cornstarch, and sugar. Pour over chicken. If there is not enough juice, add whichever liquid you prefer to bring up to the desired level. (REMEMBER THOUGH: For each extra cup of liquid, stir in another Tablespoon of cornstarch before you pour it in the slow cooker).

2. Cover and cook 6 to 8 hours on LOW. I sometimes vary the recipe, using fruit cocktail and a bit less sugar, pineapple, or apricot preserves or orange marmalade works too. (no cornstarch needed when you used preserves, nor sugar of

*course. Use your imagination. Remember sweet and sour is basically a fruit juice and vinegar.*

# Easy Cheesy Slow Cooker Chicken

### INGREDIENTS

- 6 boneless chicken breast halves, without skin • salt and pepper, to taste
- garlic powder, to taste • 2 cans condensed cream of chicken soup • 1 can condensed cheddar cheese soup

### PREPARATION

1. Rinse chicken and sprinkle with salt, pepper and garlic powder. Mix undiluted soup and pour over chicken in a Crock Pot.
2. Cover and cook on low 6 to 8 hours.
3. Serve over rice or noodles.
4. Serves 6.

# Easy Chicken Cacciatore

### INGREDIENTS

- 1 chicken, cut up, about 3 to 3 1/2 pounds •
- chopped onions • sliced mushrooms • and pepper • red pepper flakes

### PREPARATION

1 jar spaghetti sauce chopped green pepper • salt

1. Place a whole cut-up chicken (3 to 3 1/2 pounds) in the slow cooker/Crock Pot. Dump in a jar of spaghetti sauce, some cut up onions, mushrooms and green peppers. Salt and pepper to taste. (I use those little red pepper flakes too.)
2. Cook all day on low (7 to 9 hours). Serve over noodles or spaghetti.

# *Conclusion*

Thank you again for purchasing this book!
I hope this book was able to help you discover some amazing Crock Pot Recipes. The next step is to get cooking!!!

www.ingramcontent.com/pod-product-compliance
Lightning Source LLC
Chambersburg PA
CBHW070920080526
44589CB00013B/1377